Exploring the Science of

**LIGHT**

expl**O**ratorium®

Exploring the Science of

expl**O**ratorium®

# LIGHT

## 30+ Illuminating Experiments & Colorful Science Activities

weldon**owen**

# Contents

# How to Use This Book

We made this book to shed some light on light itself! At the Exploratorium, we observe and investigate the full spectrum of science daily—from physics to chemistry, biology to human behavior—and some of our most popular exhibits help visitors explore the concepts of light and color. So consider this book your ticket over the rainbow!

To best learn about the physics of light and the optics of how we see it, we've selected some of our favorite activities that Exploratorium teachers, scientists, and artists have developed over the years. Here's how they work:

**THE STEPS**

For every activity, there are step-by-step instructions and diagrams to help you make the science happen. But we encourage you to tweak these experiments to explore what interests you—each one is just a starting point for your own personal discoveries.

**TRY THIS NEXT!**

Sometimes one thing just leads to another. For some activities, we've provided fun ideas for further investigations.

**ALL THE COLORS IN THE RAINBOW**

We've also included profiles on each of the spectrum's hues, so you can learn about what makes the sky blue, carrots orange, and the planet Mars red.

**YOU'LL NEED**

Everything you need to do an activity is listed inside these circles.

**WHAT'S THE DEAL?**

These circles give you the lowdown on the facts behind the fun, explaining all the physical laws and weird science underlying the book's activities.

# Tool Kit

A handful of everyday things—which is probably lying around your home right now—helps you do the activities in this book. A few require some basic electronics; for those, you can make a quick trip to a hobbyist shop or visit an online retailer. Assemble all your tools in a box so that they'll be right there when you need them.

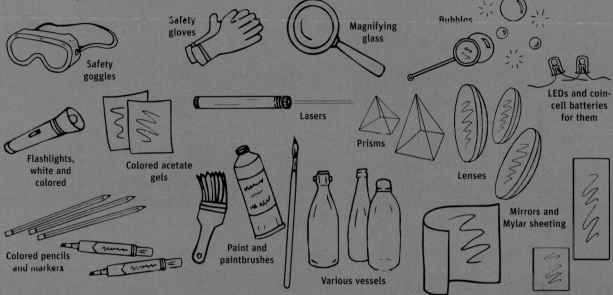

Safety gloves

Magnifying glass

Bubbles

Safety goggles

LEDs and coin-cell batteries for them

Lasers

Prisms

Flashlights, white and colored

Colored acetate gels

Lenses

Colored pencils and markers

Paint and paintbrushes

Various vessels

Mirrors and Mylar sheeting

# A Word for Parents

The activities in this book are designed for kids eight and older. The Exploratorium and the publisher have made every effort to ensure that the information and instructions included here are accurate, reliable, and mind-blowingly cool, but keep your own child's skills and attention span in mind before allowing him or her to try them, and provide supervision as needed. We disclaim all liability for any unintended, unforeseen, or improper application of the suggestions in this book, as well as any stained T-shirts or spilled bubble juice. But we're happy to accept partial credit for your kid's ever-increasing awesomeness, of course!

## About the Exploratorium

Since Frank Oppenheimer opened
the Exploratorium in 1969, we've
been an interactive learning
lab—a hands-on, playful place
to discover and to tinker—and our
thought-provoking exhibits and
programs have ignited curiosity
and delighted visitors far and
wide. At our home at Pier 15 on
San Francisco's Embarcadero,
we host more than 600 exhibits,
where visitors can dance with
their shadows; build art-making
machines; play with magnets,
pendulums, and pulleys; and
watch the ever-shifting sands
and tides of the Bay.

# Basics
# of Light

# What Is Light?

## Light makes the world visible, but there's more to it than meets the eye.

Flip on a light switch and presto—you can see! That's thanks to light, a visible type of *electromagnetic energy*. This energy comes to us from the Sun and other sources in packets called *photons*. But not all this energy is visible (such as radio waves, microwaves, X-rays, and infrared and ultraviolet light).

All of the Sun's energy travels in *waves*. Kind of like the waves at the beach, these waves have a high point (called a *crest*) and a low point (a *trough*). They can be long with lots of space between peaks, or more squished with peaks one right after another.

The distance between crests is called a *wavelength*, and the number of times that a wave cycles per second is called its *frequency*; if a wavelength is long, its frequency will be low, and vice versa. Measured in *nanometers* (a unit of measure that's equivalent to one-billionth of a meter), wavelength is a very important distance: It determines if we can see a wave or if it sneaks past our eyes undetected.

Waves with wavelengths between 390 and 700 nanometers exist in what physicists call the visible spectrum—also known as light. It includes light from the Sun or from the overhead lamp you switched on, and

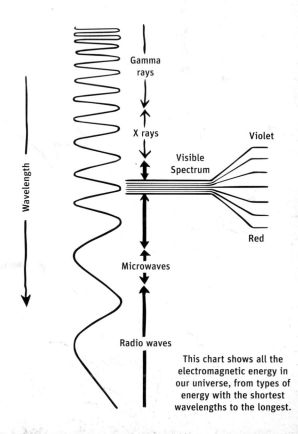

Wavelength

Gamma rays

X rays

Visible Spectrum

Microwaves

Radio waves

Violet

Red

This chart shows all the electromagnetic energy in our universe, from types of energy with the shortest wavelengths to the longest.

the combination of all these wavelengths look white to our eyes. But the wavelengths actually make up all the colors of the rainbow: red, orange, yellow, green, blue, indigo, and violet (called ROYGBIV for short).

**We only see** these colors, however, when they are separated from white light into a rainbow, as in the photo below, or when wavelengths of one color hit an object and are either reflected or absorbed by that object, making it visible and giving it color.

**Once light lands** on Earth, it behaves in fascinating ways to help us see the world around us. Turn the page to learn more.

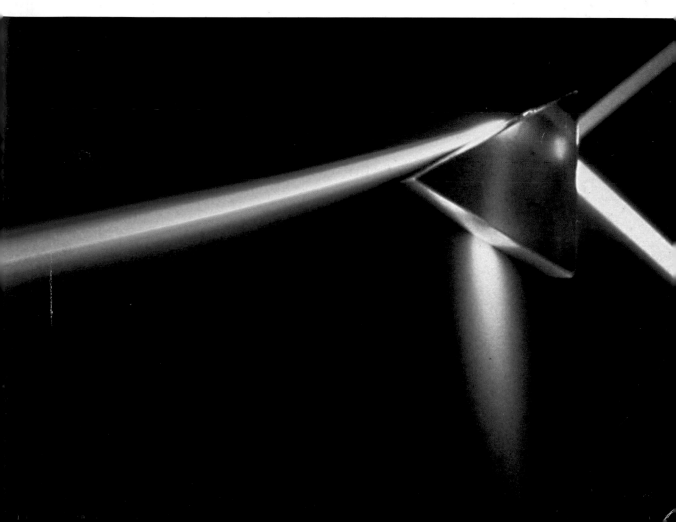

**1** **Light can be blocked.** Hold your hand between a lamp and a wall, about 2 inches (5 cm) from the wall. Since light travels in straight lines, your hand will interrupt its waves and cast a dark, crisp shadow, called an *umbra.* Move your hand farther away to see a *penumbra,* the softer, less dark area surrounding the umbra that forms when the lamp's light waves have room to spread out and hit your hand from many angles. Some waves are blocked; others sneak past. This results in a larger, fuzzier shadow.

**2** **Light can be bent.** Pour yourself a glass of water and stick a pencil in it, then look at it from the side. The pencil will appear broken at the water's surface! That's because the light coming from the underwater portion of the pencil moves more slowly than the light coming from the portion of the pencil above the water. This light is *refracted* (bent) as it travels through the liquid.

**3** **Light is absorbed.** Every object you see is absorbing some light waves while reflecting others. Your red T-shirt, for instance, is absorbing light waves of every color of the visible spectrum except red. Why, you ask? That red shirt is made of *atoms* (the basic unit of all stuff), and they contain *electrons.* Each electron has a frequency at which it naturally vibrates, and when light with the same frequency hits that electron, the light is absorbed.

**4** **Light can be bounced.** For objects to be visible at all, they can't just absorb light—they must reflect some of it, too. Mirrors are probably the most familiar light-bouncers we see, reflecting almost all the light waves that hit them. A flat, smooth mirror reflects light back at the same angle at which it first hit, creating a *specular reflection*—the kind in which a clear image of your face can be detected. Your red shirt, however, exhibits *diffuse reflection* when it reflects red light back to your eyes. That's because the shirt is rough compared to the mirror, so light is bounced back at different angles.

**5** **Light can be transmitted.** Sit by the window, and you'll see light streaming through the glass. The glass is *transmitting* light: The light doesn't contain enough energy to excite the electrons in the atoms in the glass, so they don't absorb it. Instead, they let the energy pass right through.

**6** **Light can be scattered.** Ever wonder what makes the sky blue? It's caused by *Rayleigh scattering,* in which light is spread by particles that are smaller than the wavelength of that light. Blue light has a super-short wavelength, so the teeny-tiny gas molecules of our atmosphere like to scatter it best, and as a result our sky is a heavenly hue of blue.

# How Light Behaves

Light has all sorts of neat tricks that
you can observe all around you.

# Seeing Is Believing

## Now that you know a little about light, let's learn how our eyes use it to see.

**Eyes are pretty incredible.** They've evolved over a few hundred million years to show us our world. When you open up your peepers first thing in the morning, light streams in through your *pupil*: the small hole at the center of the colored part of your eye (which is called the *iris*). This hole appears black, and the iris moves to control how much light enters it. (For example, when light is low, the iris contracts to expose more of your pupil, letting in more illumination so that you can see.)

**Once the light** has made it past your eye's pupil, it goes through a *lens*—a clear, colorless bit of tissue. It's the lens's job to focus the light on the back of your eyeball so that all the light rays reflected from the same point meet in one spot. To do so, the lens subtly changes its shape to bend the light and focus just the right amount on an area called the *retina*.

**You can think** of the retina as the movie screen of your eye: The lens projects the light onto this surface, creating an upside down image of the world outside, which we call a

*pinhole* image. It occurs because light from outside that is higher than your pupil travels in a straight line to the lower half of the back of your eye, while light that is lower travels to the upper half of the back of your eye.

**So how come** the world doesn't look upside down to you? That's because the cells in the retina in the back of your eye detect the image, and then your brain flips it

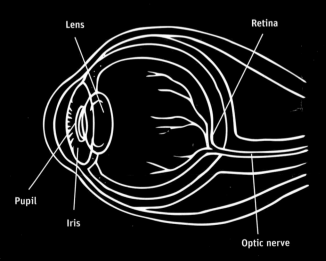

Lens

Retina

Pupil

Iris

Optic nerve

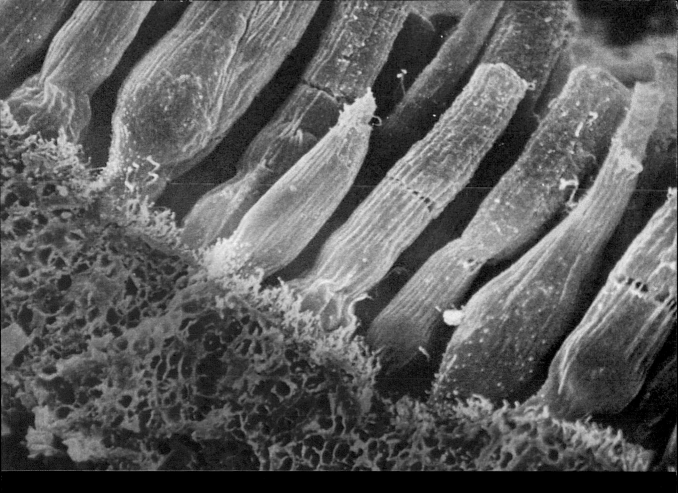

back. The cells in your retina are called *rods* and *cones* (pictured above using a scanning electron microscope). The rods are sensitive to all wavelengths of visible light, while the three types of cone cells are each sensitive to a different color of light: red, green, or blue.

**Together, rods and cones** work to process what your eye sees, creating a three-dimensional, full-color view of the world. Once they've gathered all the information, they zip the news along the *optic nerve* to the visual cortex in your brain, where the upside-down image on the back of your retina is finally flipped right side up, and you're able to understand the shape, size, texture, details, and colors of what you see. Pretty neat!

# Exploring
# Light

Observe sunspots and streaks in the wild
with a few simple perforated cards.

# Go on a Light Walk

1. **Start by making** what we call a spots-and-streaks card, shown at left. Download the template at www.exploratorium.edu/exploring-light and print it out, then use it as a guide to cut 3/16-inch- (5-mm-) diameter square, round, triangular, and star-shaped holes in your cardboard with a craft knife. Add a slightly larger square hole about 3/8 inch (9.5 mm) in diameter. Cut two perpendicular slits 3/16 inch by 2 inches (5 mm by 5 cm).

2. **Next, you need** what we call an array-of-holes card. Again, download and print out the template, then use your craft knife to cut a grid of 3/16-inch- (5-mm-) across square holes in the manila folder, 3/4 inch (2 cm) apart.

3. **Take to the streets** with your folder, posterboard, and friend. First, hold the spots-and-streaks card about 1 foot (30 cm) away from your posterboard and let the sunlight pass through its holes—adjust its position so that the spots are round. Then move it toward

## What's the Deal?

Every time the Sun shines through your cardboard holes, you are isolating tiny images of the Sun. These images appear oval when the sunlight is shining on the ground at an angle—but when you hold your posterboard perpendicular to the Sun's rays, the spots become round.

the Sun—once you're more than 6 feet (1.8 m) from the posterboard, the spots will still be round, but larger holes and the slits will make long streaks. Use your fingers to divide a slit into smaller, circular images.

4. **Use your array-of-holes** card to make a grid of Sun images on the posterboard. As you move the card away, the circular images will overlap. Use tape to make some holes smaller, and let the Sun shine through the card. Notice a change to the size and brightness of the images?

## Try This Next!

This activity was developed by Bob Miller, an Exploratorium exhibit designer and artist who led troops of curious folks on light walks. He loved to demonstrate how any simple spot of sunlight shows the Sun's angle and intensity—make your hand into a loose fist or crisscross your fingers so light streams through the gaps, and you'll see tons of little suns, similar to sunlight dappling through a tree's leaves.

## What's the Deal?

Your shadow goes everywhere you do, so you've surely noticed that it morphs throughout the day. Your toy's shadow is no different! In the morning, the Sun is low in the eastern sky, so the toy's shadow lengthens and points more toward the west. As the Earth turns, the Sun appears to rise in the sky and move west, making the toy's shadow get shorter and move in the opposite direction. As the Sun sets in the west, the shadow points east and grows longer until it disappears in the dark. The cool thing about this? It's a clue to a puzzle that people took thousands of years to solve: Earth spins like a top, and it orbits around the Sun (that's called *heliocentrism*). This rotation happens every day, and it makes the Sun appear to be moving across the sky—but our planet is the one that's revolving!

**1** **Early on a sunny day,** place your toy on the sidewalk and outline its shadow with chalk. Note the time on your watch.

**2** **Wait an hour** and outline its shadow with a new color of chalk. Did the shadow get longer? Shorter? Is it the same size as the toy? Is it squashed or more defined?

**3** **Keep tracing the shadow** at one-hour intervals. After a while, you'll have a colorful fan or starburst shape of shadows on the sidewalk.

### Try This Next!

Once you've documented your toy's shifting shadow, try tracking the shade cast by larger and more elaborate structures, like the power-line tower you see here. (If the shadow falls in the grass, map its movement by sticking small sticks in the ground and connecting them with colored string.)

# The Rad Shadow Sketch

Grab a favorite toy and turn its shadow into art that illustrates an ancient solar-system secret.

**You'll need:**

A sunny day

Stretch of peaceful sidewalk without a lot of foot traffic

Tall toy with an interesting shape or silhouette

Packet of sidewalk chalk

A watch

Small sticks

Colored string

Shadows aren't always black.
Colorful ones are extra fun!

# Colored Shadows

**1** **First, you need** three flashlights in red, green, and blue. Give two of the flashlights to your friends and snag one for yourself.

**2** **Kill the room lights.** Line up in front of a white wall, with the green flashlight in the middle, the red one to the right, and the blue one to the left. The person with the green light aims it straight at the wall; the blue and red flashlight wielders slant their lights so that they hit the same area as the green light. Mysteriously, this should create white light.

**3** **Hold your free hands** between the flashlights and the wall. Adjust your distance until each hand casts three distinct shadows in cyan, magenta, and yellow. Move your hands to overlap their shadows and watch which hues appear in the intersecting areas.

**4** **Now block one flashlight.** Repeat the experiment with a different light turned off while the other two remain on, and then repeat a third time so that you've tried all the combinations. How many colors can you make?

**5** **Keep playing,** mixing up the order of the flashlights and holding up objects with interesting shapes, such as the film reel here. Or try a few acrobatic moves to see colored shadows in action.

## What's the Deal?

The retina of the human eye has three types of receptors for colored light: One each for red, green, and blue. When the three lights shine on the wall, all three types of color receptors are stimulated, giving us the sensation of white. Red, green, and blue are therefore called *additive primaries* of light. But if you block one of the three lights, you get a shadow that's a mix of the two other colors. If the blue and green mix, they make cyan; red and blue make magenta; and red and green make yellow. When you overlap shadows, you block two beams, and blue, red, or green shadows emerge. And when you block all three beams, the shadows go black!

# Shadowbox Theater

**Found materials cast mesmerizing shapes in your own personal shadow show.**

**1** Cut away your box's bottom—this will be your theater's front. Open the box's other end and set the box on one side, then tape paper or a sheet over the cut-away opening. You can reinforce the box's sides with dowels or yardsticks.

**2** Darken the room and turn on a flashlight. (For an extra-strong beam, try unscrewing the flashlight's cover.) Secure the flashlight so that it shines through the screen. Tape the "on" button down for continuous lighting.

### What's the Deal?

Shadow theaters have been around for more than 1,000 years, and they're still a beautiful way to learn about light. By experimenting with various objects, you're able to observe how they block, bounce, diffuse, or filter its rays. You'll also notice how objects that are close to the screen cast small, crisp shapes, while farther objects appear large though fuzzy. And if you aim a light through a colored, transparent object, you'll see its shape and splendid hues projected, too.

**3** Now's the time to try out a shadow-maker! Grab one—say, a colander—and ask your friend to stand in front of the screen and report what she sees. Keeping your body out of the light, hold up the colander inside the back of the box, experimenting with moving it closer to and farther from the light. Switch with your friend so you can see, too!

**4** Try more objects. What kind of shadows will a colored glass of water make? What about a crystal, lace, toys, or strawberry baskets? Try bubble wrap, transparencies printed with designs, or mirrors, too.

**5** Add colored flashlights to see how they affect the images on your screen. (You can also tape colored acetate gels over your flashlights.) What if you try moving the objects—rotating them or fastening them to wire or dowels like puppets? Can you use objects to tell a story, such as the underwater scene here?

**You'll need:**

Large cardboard box

Scissors

Tape

A screen—this could be a piece of white paper, white plastic bag, or white sheet

Dowels or yardsticks

A room you can darken

Strong single-LED flashlights, white and colored

A bunch of objects to cast shadows—look for stuff with texture, transparency, holes, and interesting shapes

A friend

An audience!

Capture your very own spectrum
of color in a water spray.

# Backyard Rainbows

1. Sunlight enters
a water drop . . .

2. bends and
separates . . .

3. and bounces
off the back of
the drop . . .

Violet

4. fanning out into a rainbow!

Red

1. **Ask a friend** to hold the hose while you face the fine spray or mist with your back to the sun. Your shadow should be in front of you, in the middle of the spray. (It helps to face a dark background.)

2. **Find your rainbow!** If you don't see it right away, look for the shadow of your head. Hold both arms straight out in front of you, spread your hands wide with your thumb tips touching, then extend the tip of one pinky finger so that its shadow lands in the center of your head's shadow. Hold that pinky where it is and look at the sunlit drops lined up with your other pinky—you should see your own personal rainbow!

## What's the Deal?

You see a rainbow in the hose's spray because light *refracts,* or bends, when it travels from air into water—or anything transparent, for that matter. Once inside the water drop, light bounces off the sphere's far side, then bends again on its way out. But sunlight is made up of all the colors of the spectrum, and each bends at a slightly different angle. So when the light passes through the water, the colors separate and fan out into the vivid, many-hued arc that we love to see.

3. **Move around a bit** and see how your personal rainbow moves with you. Get a few friends or family members set up with more personal rainbows, then ask everyone to point to the top of their rainbow—you'll all be pointing in different places.

## Try This Next!

Keep your eyes peeled for the unicorn of all rainbows—the double rainbow! This elusive sight is the result of light reflecting twice inside a droplet of water. It'll appear as a bigger, fainter rainbow outside the smaller, brighter primary one, and you'll notice something funny about the order of the colors. In the primary rainbow, the color goes from red on the outside to violet on the inside (your typical ROYGBIV), but in the secondary one, violet will be on the outside with red on the inside. Can you say VIBGYOR?!

# Red

First up on our tour of the visible spectrum is red. With a wavelength between 620 and 740 nanometers, red has the longest wavelength and the lowest frequency of any color. But red is more than just physics—it's the color of blood, flames, and flushed cheeks. Seeing the color red often makes us stop and pay attention.

Scientists have observed red's specific effect on human psychology: It makes us hungry! Red coloration tells us when fruit is ripe and meat is fresh enough to eat, making our stomachs rumble—the reason fast-food restaurants put red in their logos.

Hunger

Why does the planet Mars look red to us? Because it's covered with a layer of iron oxide, or rust. Sometime in the last few billion years, a bunch of iron on Mars's surface interacted with oxygen to make that rusty red.

Cochineal

A lot of red stuff owes its color to bugs. The cochineal is a tiny insect native to Latin America that produces a molecule called carminic acid to ward off predators. Dating back to the Aztec and Mayan empires, people have used it in dye baths for textiles, like you see here. Today, it's mostly used to color cosmetics and food. That's right, you may be eating bugs!

Mars

A red tide is a nicer nickname for what scientists call a *harmful algal bloom*. It's caused by algae growing at a bonkers rate near the water's surface, and it gets its alarming rusty hue from the algae's photosynthetic material. A red tide can kill fish and fill shellfish with toxins, making them dangerous to eat. So beware the sunset in the sea.

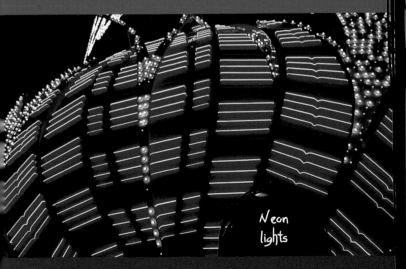

**Red tide**

**Red-green color blindness**

Imagine seeing green leaves as a dull yellow-gray—that's what people with red-green color blindness see. There are many types of color blindness, but this particular disorder affects the eye's red and green color receptors, the genes for which are carried on the X chromosome. Women with this disorder have this deficiency on both X chromosomes, but men only need it on their solo X chromosome to get confused at traffic lights.

**Neon lights**

Neon: It lights the way to the nearest superstar on stage or cold soda on the corner. But it's also an example of a group of elements called *noble gases*, which do not react very easily. When a gas gets a jolt of electricity, its electrons start bopping around and colliding, and their energy is given off as light—in the case of neon, a dazzling, long-lasting red!

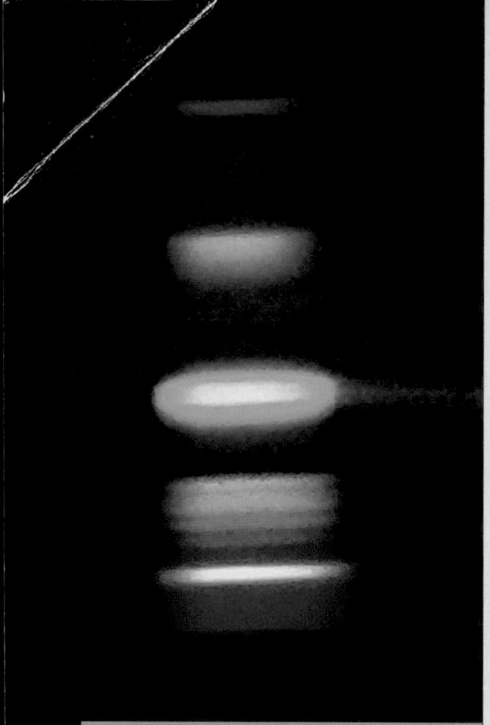

## What's the Deal?

Music is digitally recorded using a spiral track of pits on a CD's mirrored surface, encoded ones and zeros. These tracks are regularly spaced at a very small distance, so they act as a *diffraction grating* for light, meaning they spread out the light waves, separating the different colors. The CD's mirrored surface allows the light to be reflected back to your eye. Each color of light bends differently, which is why you have to look at the CD at a certain angle to be able to see the whole spectrum.

**1** Cut a straight slit in your flat cardboard circle, then tape the circle over one end of your cardboard tube.

**2** Place the tube on a surface so that the slit is horizontal and facing away from you. Near the end closest to you, cut a slot in the tube that's about ½ by ½ inch (1.25 by 1.25 cm). This is your peephole.

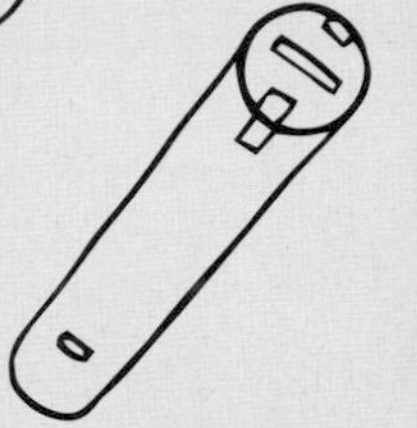

**3** Near this end of the tube, directly opposite your viewing hole, cut another thin slit at a 45-degree angle. Insert the CD into this slot.

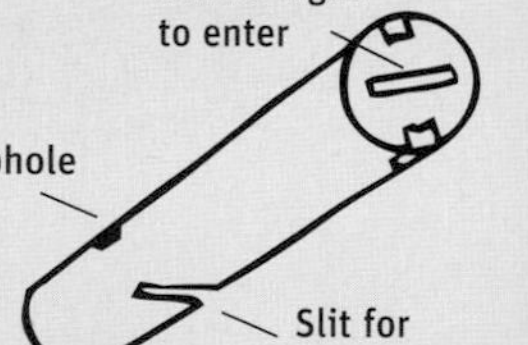

Slit for light to enter

Peephole

Slit for the CD

**4** Point the top slit at a light (never at the Sun—point it at a cloud or white piece of paper instead) and look through the peephole. You'll see the light pass through the slit and divide into a cool rainbow on the CD!

## Try This Next!

Use your *spectroscope* (this device that produces a spectrum of light from a source) to investigate any light source, including a fluorescent bulb, which produced the above image. In fluorescent light, you'll see bright, separated lines inside a continuous spectrum, which are created by mercury gas and phosphor. Meanwhile, a neon light will divide only into red or orange colors—no ROYGBIV there!—and an RGB monitor will give you three lines in the spectrum's red, green, and blue zones. You can even use a candle, in which you'll see a continuous spectrum of the incandescent carbon particles in the flame. Brilliant!

# Spectroscopes Inspect Light

## Create diffractions of light with this do-it-yourself instrument.

**You'll need:**

A circle of flat cardboard big enough to cover the end of your cardboard tube

Craft knife

Clear or masking tape

A cardboard tube that's at least 10 inches (25 cm) long—a paper towel tube works great

A CD

One or more light sources

1. Light passes through a slit in the spectroscope's covered top . . .

2. travels down the tube . . .

3. and forms a spectrum on the disk, which you can see through a hole!

# Bubbles' Incre-dubble Colors!

See amazing swirls of color on the delicate surface of soap bubbles.

## You'll need:

1 gallon (3.8 L) water

⅔ cup (150 mL) dishwashing soap

2 tablespoons glycerin

Large basin or small plastic or inflatable pool

Small hula hoop

Small, clear plastic lid

Clear tape

Flashlight

Drinking straws

Pipe cleaners

String

Black paper

Pan of water

Clear nail polish

**1** **Make a batch** of bubble juice by mixing the water, soap, and glycerin in the basin or pool. Dunk the small hula hoop into the soapy goodness. Get your hands nice and sudsy, too!

**2** **Slowly lift** the hoop, bringing it up and toward you. Watch a massive bubble form inside the hoop. When the hoop is almost out, hold it vertically to seal your big, bubbly film.

**3** **Observe the swirling rainbow** on the face of the bubble. How many colors do you count? Do they change over a few minutes? What colors do you see right before the bubble pops? Do black and white show up anywhere?

**4** **Put your hula hoop aside,** and tape the plastic lid, lip facing up, over the bulb end of the flashlight. Turn on your flashlight and hold it vertically.

**5** **With your finger,** take a little bubble juice and dab it on the lid to wet it. Then put a spoonful of bubble juice on the lid, forming a little pool. With a straw, very gently blow a bubble so that you create a dome covering the whole lid.

Turn the page ⟹

### Try This Next!

Next time it rains, keep your eyes on the street for oil slick rainbows—beautiful colors caused by the amplification or cancellation of light waves as they reflect from the layers of oil and water. You can re-create this effect by submerging a piece of black paper in a pan of water, dripping clear nail polish on the water's surface, then lifting the paper out. The nail polish will spread into a thin layer on the paper, leaving you an iridescent, colorific display—a permanent oil slick!

## What's the Deal?

Here's a scientist's secret for you:
A bubble's delicate membrane is actually a sandwich, with a layer of soap molecules on either side of a layer of water molecules. When light waves reflecting off the front soap layer meet waves reflecting off the back soap layer, the waves can meet each other crest-to-crest, adding up and reinforcing the waves' color (which is called *constructive interference*), or they can meet crest-to-trough, canceling each other out (known as *destructive interference*). In this second scenario, you see the wave's complementary color. The color shifts result from the ever-changing thickness of the bubble's filmy shell. The bubble solution will get thinner until no light is reflected and black replaces the vividly colored bands, until the bubble is so thin that only a few moments remain until . . .
POP!

Straw

Bubble over the flashlight's dome

Flashlight

**6** **Turn off the lights** and hold the flashlight so the lid is just above your eyes. Look up—what colors and shapes do you see?

**7** **Now grab your pipe cleaners** and straws. Fold a pipe cleaner into thirds to form joints, then slide the straws over the folded pipe cleaners. Connect your straws into different geometric shapes—try tetrahedrons or cubes!—and tie strings to them.

**8** **Dip the frames** so they're completely submerged in the bubble juice, then hold them up to the light. Again, watch the colors form. How do they differ from the bubbles in the hula hoop and over the flashlight?

To form the joints of the geometric shapes, fold a pipe cleaner . . .

. . . then slip straws over the folds.

# Never Dreary Color Theory

## Think red, blue, and yellow are the primary colors? Think again!

**You'll need:**

Finger or acrylic paint in a bunch of colors

Large white surface (paper works)

A blending instrument—your finger will do!

Color photo

Magnifying glass

1. **Survey your paint selection** for three specific colors: Cyan (a blue-green), yellow, and magenta. Place a dab of each in a large triangle on the paper, leaving plenty of space between the dots for color mixing to spread out.

2. **Let's make more colors!** Mix a bit of magenta with cyan halfway between those two dabs. Then mix cyan with yellow, then magenta with yellow. You should now see smears of bold blue, vivid green, and brick red interspersed with your original triangle. (You may have to play with the ratios to get the colors just right, but trust us, they're in there!)

3. **Keep mixing,** and a color wheel will appear on your surface. You've uncovered the CMYK (cyan-magenta-yellow-key [black]) spectrum, which is used in all color printing.

## What's the Deal?

Mixing color pigments, like the ones in paint, works differently than mixing light. When colored light appears on a computer screen, for example, it functions *additively*, meaning that combining red, green, and blue light will create almost all other colors and, ultimately, white light. By contrast, you see different shades in your paints because they absorb some colors and reflect others from white light; hence, some colors are "subtracted" from white light. In this model, the primary colors of pigment aren't red, blue, and yellow as you learned in school, but instead are cyan, magenta, and yellow because they combine to make almost all colors, plus black.

4. **Mix a little bit** of cyan, magenta, and yellow again, this time all in one small spot. What color emerges?

### Try This Next!

Peer at a color photograph through a magnifying glass, and you'll see tiny flecks of color that, when seen at a distance, blur together to look like lots of colors. These uniform spots will be—you guessed it—cyan, magenta, yellow, or black (a combo of the first three).

## What's the Deal?

A red filter transmits mostly red light and absorbs all other colors—so a picture containing red, green, and blue looks red and black under a red filter. (As you can guess, a green filter transmits mostly green light, and a blue filter transmits mostly blue light.) And if you look at a partially peeled banana through a red filter? The white banana and the yellow peel will look red, because white and yellow pigment reflect some red light. Similarly, when you view multicolored letters or sketches through a red filter, some red marks disappear because they blend in with the red light reflected by the white paper. Other shapes, such as the frog on the next page, reflect no red light and stand out as green!

**1** Take a piece of white paper and write a message on it, using a different color crayon, colored pencil, or marker for each letter.

**2** Look at the design on the paper through a red filter. Which letters vanish, and which ones can you see? The red filter should make any red letters mysteriously vanish, while all the other letters should even more mysteriously show up as black! If you use crayons, it may take some experimentation to find a red color that vanishes perfectly with your red filter.

**3** Try the experiment again using different colors of filters and differently colored crayons, markers, or pencils. And what happens when you look through two filters at once, such as magenta and cyan or red and blue? (You should see blue and black, respectively.) What colors do you get if you hold up three filters at once?

**4** Once you've figured out which colors you can see through various filters, try writing a top-secret message or making a highly hush-hush drawing in a color that shows up when seen through the filter— such as the one you see to the right—then scribble or doodle around or over it with the other colors so that your message is hidden to the unaided eye. Then pass the paper and filter to a friend in the know!

# Reveal Secret Messages

A colored filter transmits some colors and absorbs others. Use one to create and decode secret images!

## You'll need:

White paper

Colored crayons, pencils, markers, or pens

A few sheets of transparent plastic in bright colors such as red, green, and blue*

Pictures from a magazine or book

*Look for colored acetate report covers, acrylic plastic sheets, or even colored plastic wrap.

# Orange

Eye-catching orange comes second on the spectrum, with a wavelength between 590 and 620 nanometers. It gets its name from the tasty citrus, but its hues aren't limited to the produce section: We see it in the sky, foliage, minerals, safety gear, and more! It's also crucial to the world's worst joke: Orange you glad I didn't say banana?

You might think astronauts have really limited fashion sense, but the orange suits they wear during takeoff and landing have a major safety purpose. If something goes wrong and the astronauts need to be rescued, orange is the easiest color to spot from above by land or by sea.

Astronaut suits

Vividly colored saffron comes from the saffron crocus and has been used as a spice, medication, and pigment for thousands of years. For each violet crocus blossom, there are only three orange filaments.

Sunsets

Sunsets appear in shades of orange because only longer wavelengths such as yellow, orange, and red penetrate the atmosphere when the sun is low. This angle results in sunlight passing through more of the atmosphere, which scatters and filters shorter wavelengths such as green, blue, and violet until just reds, oranges, and yellows make it to your eyes.

Saffron

Carrots

Did you know that this burnt-orange gemstone was tree resin millions of years ago? Over time it hardened, and its simple molecules began to join into larger, more complex, stable molecules in a process known as *polymerization*. Eventually, the substance completely polymerizes, sometimes preserving bugs and leaves that got caught in the sap!

Amber

Have you ever seen a baby who likes eating cooked carrots so much that it literally turns him orange? This isn't an illusion: It actually is possible to eat so many carrots that you take on their hue. *Carotene* is a pigment found in carrots, and if you eat enough, you'll develop *carotenemia*, which (while harmless) will turn you orange, starting with your palms and nose.

Autumn leaves

You've probably heard of *chlorophyll,* the chemical that makes plants green and enables *photosynthesis*, or the conversion of light to energy. When it starts to get cold, trees adapt to the fact that there soon won't be enough light for photosynthesis. The green chlorophyll disappears, revealing red and orange hues that were there all along, obscured by the chlorophyll.

See what colors lurk inside your everyday black marker.

# Unpack Black with Color Chromatography

1. **Cut a strip** of absorbent paper the size of a bookmark: 2 by 6 inches (6 by 15 cm).

2. **Take a marker** and draw a thick line on the strip parallel to the short side, making sure that it's 1 to 2 inches (2.5—5 cm) from the bottom.

3. **Put just a little water** in your glass, then dunk the strip's marked end in the water. Don't dunk the mark itself! To hold the strip in place, fold the clean end over the glass's side and secure with a clip.

4. **Check out the water** seeping up the paper strip—it'll reach the black line and then you'll see more colors spreading up.

5. **Hang tight** until the colors reach the top of the strip, then survey your tracks of color. How many hues do you see separated out of the initial black mark? Did any of them travel farther out on the strip than others?

6. **Extra credit:** Take a different brand of water-based black marker and try the experiment again. Are the colors different?

## What's the Deal?

Your water-soluble marker is made of colored pigments and water. When you draw with it, the ink carries the pigment onto the paper, and then the water in the ink dries, leaving just the pigment. But when you dunked your paper strip, water traveled back into the paper to your original mark and dissolved the dried pigment. The watercolor effect is created by the different pigment molecules in the marker, which separate and travel at different rates due to their size, how well they dissolve in water, and how well they stick to the paper.

① **Download a disk template** at www.exploratorium.edu/exploring-light and print it out. (You may need to experiment with printing it at a size that will fit your rotator.) If the black doesn't come out solid, use a black marker to fill in any grayish areas.

② **Mount the disk** on the posterboard or cardboard with the glue stick.

③ **Fasten the patterned disk** to your rotator. If your rotator is a top, tape the disk in place; if it's a pencil, stick a pushpin through the disk's center and then into the eraser. As always, get creative and stay safe.

④ **Get under** a bright incandescent light or outside in the sun—fluorescent beams will work in a pinch, but they will make the disk pulsate. Trippy!

## What's the Deal?

Invented by toy maker Charles Benham in 1895, this spinning wonder's mysterious effect involves the red-, green-, and blue-sensitive cells in our eyes, called *cones*. When you watch the spinning disk, you see alternating flashes of black and white. On the white flashes, all three cone types respond, but your eyes only tell your brain "white!" when all three types respond equally. But some cones respond quicker or for longer than others, creating the perception of colors. Plus, the black bands have different lengths that flash at different rates, so you may see color bands varying across the disk.

⑤ **Spin the disk** and observe the colored bands that appear. In what order do the colors show up? What color do you see at the center? What happens when you reverse the spin or try a different speed?

⑥ **Design your own disks.** What kind of colors can you trick your eyes into seeing?

## Try This Next!

Explore the flip side of Benham's disk—Newton's disk! On thick posterboard, make a wheel containing all seven colors of the rainbow. Place this disk on the spinning top and give it a go—what do you see? The colors should smear to white! This is how, in 1672, Sir Isaac Newton famously demonstrated that white light is made up of different colors, and defined the spectrum of light.

# See Colors Spin in a Black-and-White Disk

## Give Benham's disk a whirl—and let its hidden colors amaze you.

**You'll need:**

Black-and-white disk from
www.exploratorium.edu/exploring-light

Printer and printer paper

Black marker

Stiff paper, such as posterboard
or cardboard

Glue stick

Rotator—a toy top, a pencil with eraser,
or a spinner of your own invention!

Colored markers

# The Mesmerizing
# Picture Mixer

Smash two images together with a DIY thaumatrope.

1. **Draw a circle** onto an index card, then cut it out and trace the shape onto your second index card. Cut it out, too.

2. **Hold the disks** back-to-back. Punch two holes in them, one right across from the other.

3. **Draw a simple picture,** such as a stick figure carrying an umbrella, in the middle of the first disk.

4. **Take the second disk** and put it on top of the first one so that the holes line up. Making sure you can see the first drawing through the paper (put some light behind it if the paper is too thick), draw a corresponding image on the second disk—such as raindrops for your stick man.

5. **Flip the second card over** so that the blank back of the first disk meets the blank back of the second disk, and the holes match up again. Glue the disks together.

6. **Take a piece of string** (or a cut-open rubber band) and thread it through one of the holes. Tie a small knot close to the hole. Repeat with another piece of string on the other hole.

7. **Hold the strings taut** and roll them between your thumbs and forefingers to see what happens. As if by magic, the man with the umbrella will appear to be marching through the rain!

## What's the Deal?

From the Greek, *thauma* means "magic," and *trope* is something that turns. Thus, the thaumatrope creates spinning illusions: You spin it and the two images on either side seem to merge. This is because your mind tends to see an image for a fraction of a second longer than the image appears (called *persistence of vision*). The cells in your eyes are undergoing a chemical reaction, and during this delay they're not able to clearly discern a superquick change in light. As a result, your eyes combine the two images. Believe it or not, this optic toy helped lead to the invention of movies!

**1** **With the craft knife,** completely remove the tops of the milk cartons. Then, near the bottom of one milk carton, cut a rectangular hole about ¼ inch (6.35 mm) in from either side of the carton. This is your peephole.

**2** **Next up,** make a slot for a mirror. Flip the carton on its long side so that the hole you just made faces to the right. On the side now facing up, measure 2¾ inches (7 cm) from the bottom of the carton on its left side. Make a mark there, then use your ruler to draw a straight diagonal line from this mark to the bottom right corner.

**3** **Hold your mirror** along this line and mark its length. Then use the craft knife to cut a slit as long as your mirror, using the line as a guide.

**4** **Pop the mirror** into its new slot with the reflective side facing out the hole. Tape it in place on the side.

**5** **Hold the carton** to your eye and look through the peephole—you should see the ceiling! If the ceiling looks tilted, adjust the mirror. Repeat these steps with the second milk carton.

**6** **Stand one carton** with the bottom hole facing you; hold the other above it facing the opposite position, with the hole at the top facing away from you. Pinch this carton's sides slightly and slide it into the top of the carton. Tape the two cartons together at the seam.

**7** **Get your spy on!** Look through the top hole to see under tables and beds; look through the bottom hole to see over fences, older siblings, and tall buildings. Hold it sideways to see around corners!

## What's the Deal?

*Periscopes* work because light reflects away from a mirror at the same angle that it hits it: It hits the top mirror at 45 degrees and reflects it away at 45 degrees, then hits the second mirror at 45 degrees, reflects away from the second mirror at 45 degrees, and then finally it hits your eye. That's why a periscope helps us see things that normally wouldn't be in our field of vision—above our heads, under a table, or around a corner. Submarines use this same technology, only their periscopes have to be very long (and include a series of magnifying lenses) to see over the surface of the water from the ocean's depths.

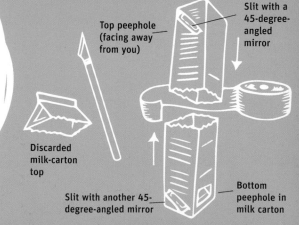

Top peephole (facing away from you)

Slit with a 45-degree-angled mirror

Discarded milk-carton top

Slit with another 45-degree-angled mirror

Bottom peephole in milk carton

Peek around corners, under sofas, and over fences—all with stealthy light-wave geometry.

# Up Periscope!

## You'll need:

2 empty, rinsed 1-quart (950-mL) milk cartons

Craft knife

Ruler

Pencil or pen

2 identical small plastic pocket mirrors, ideally ones that are square and flat

Sturdy tape

# Double Your Fun with Hinged Mirrors

**Manipulating mirrors makes stupendous symmetry.**

**You'll need:**

Two equal-size mirrors

Duct tape

Construction paper

Markers, pens, pencils, or other writing utensils

Glitter, jewels, or other fun, reflective craft materials

Protractor

1. **Position your two mirrors** so that their faces touch, and fasten them together along one edge with duct tape. Bingo—there's your hinged mirror.

2. **Using your paper,** markers, glitter, and other craft materials, make some awesome shapes, scribbles, and other fun designs. Whatever you place under the mirror will be reflected across the hinge, so play with patterns and shapes that will look neat when multiplied.

3. **Set your hinged mirrors** on top of the patterns you just made. Whoa—they make a 360-degree design! Count the number of reflections you see.

4. **Experiment with widening** and narrowing the angle of the mirrors—you may even want to use a protractor to mark 30 degrees, 60 degrees, 90 degrees, 120 degrees, and so forth on a piece of paper under the mirrors. Then see how opening and closing the mirrors to these lines affects the reflections.

## Try This Next!

What happens when you play with hinged mirrors from above instead of below? Set up your hinged mirrors, then hold objects as simple as your hands between the mirrors and an overhead light source. Even shadows create symmetrical images of themselves in the hinged mirrors. Awesome!

## What's the Deal?

When you place an object between the two mirrors, the light hitting the object bounces back and forth between the mirrors, then hits your eyes. When light bounces off one of the mirrors, a new image is formed in *symmetry* (an image that, cut down the middle, is the same on both sides). The more symmetrical images you see, the more times light is bouncing on and off the mirrors. How many images you see depends on the angle between the mirrors: A smaller angle bounces light back and forth more times, creating more images, while a larger angle bounces light fewer times, creating fewer images.

# See Infinity in a Kaleidoscope

Hey kid, you're pretty
neat. So let's multiply
you to infinity.

1. **There's more than one way** to make your own kaleidoscope. Here, we've used three cheap plastic mirrors—such as the kind you hang on the back of your closet door—for a jumbo version. But you can use three smaller mirrors, too, as long as they're the same size. We always suggest using plastic mirrors for safety. Start by taping them together in a row with duct tape, leaving enough room for the tape to act as a hinge as they bend.

2. **Now tape the mirrors** to form an equilateral triangle. (If your mirrors are flimsy, you can cut cardboard pieces to size and tape them to the mirror backs for extra support.)

3. **Set the Kaleidoscope** on the floor and take a seat at its center, or have your grown ups hold the kaleidoscope while you duck inside and see yourself multiplied into infinite reflections! Invite some friends in on the fun, too.

4. **Add more mirrors!** You've seen how a triangle reflects your image; now untape it and add mirrors to create various closed shapes, such as a square, a rectangle, or a hexagon. Put each shape over your head, or place an object in the shape's center. How do the reflections change?

## What's the Deal?

When you stand inside your kaleidoscope, you see each mirror reflecting the images displayed in the other two mirrors. This results in a mind-bending, 360-degree display of reflections of reflections! Although kaleidoscopes were originally intended as scientific tools, they've gained popularity as toys, too.

# Yellow

When light with a wavelength between 570 and 590 nanometers passes before our eyes, we see yellow: The color of bright lemons, shiny gold, and blazing summer-time sunshine. One of the most visible colors in the spectrum, yellow immediately excites our eyes and makes us pay attention.

Pollen, simply put, is plant sperm. Tiny particles called *flavonoids* give pollen its color and protect it from harmful ultraviolet rays. Since pollen is what holds a plant's precious genetic material, these brightly colored flavonoids help flowers keep breeding and blooming.

Pollen

Since prehistoric times, yellow paint has been extracted from clay in the form of ochre pigment, making yellow one of the very first available paint color choices! We see yellow ochre paint in prehistoric cave art, such as the 20,000 year-old horse painting in the caverns of Lascaux, France. Aboriginal peoples of Australia also used yellow ochre in ceremonies.

Yellow ochre

Yellow is a high-visibility color, even in fog, rain, or darkness. That's why many roadside warning signs around the world are yellow: They catch people's eyes and make them proceed with caution.

Road signs

Sulfur is the only element in the periodic table that's naturally yellow. You can find piles of this odorless, tasteless, and brittle solid around hot springs and volcanoes. Once it teams up with other elements (such as hydrogen) to form compounds, you'll likely smell it before you see it—and it'll smell a lot like rotten eggs!

The Sun

Why does sunshine appear yellow? Sunbeams are actually white, emitting photons of all colors of light. But photons with the highest frequencies in the spectrum—blues and violets—scatter easily, meaning they get obscured by Earth's atmosphere. Lower-frequency photons such as orange and yellow don't scatter easily, so they make it through the sky to our eyes.

Sulfur

Urine

Just what makes our pee yellow, you ask? Urine is your body's way of getting rid of waste. It gets its tinge from *urobilin,* which is created when a substance called *bilirubin* breaks down. Bilirubin comes from worn-out red blood cells, and is the chemical that makes bruises look sallow. Drink a lot of water to keep your urine a healthy, light-yellow color!

A strategically placed mirror makes simple activities go completely bonkers.

# Hat Trick

1. **Tape the mirror** to the underside of the baseball cap's visor—make sure it's attached securely. Put on the cap and sit down at the table. Position yourself, the table, and the maze so that when you look up at the mirror in the cap, you can see the maze on the table.

2. **Looking up into the mirror,** take your pen or pencil and—watching your hand only in the mirror, without looking down—try to follow the maze.

3. **Once you master this,** grab a piece of paper and try to write a whole sentence, or draw a house, cat, or stick figure. Then try taking a few steps while only looking in the mirror. It's a lot harder than usual, huh?

### You'll need:

Small mirror

Masking tape

Baseball cap or other headwear with a visor

Table or desk

Maze from an activity book

Pen or pencil

Piece of paper

## What's the Deal?

When you usually write or draw, your eyes and hands work together, but in this experiment, the information you get from your eyes doesn't match the messages you get from your hand. Everything you perceive on the paper is upside down: When you try to move your hand up, the mirror will show your hand moving down—the usual signals sent by your brain are now sending your hand in the wrong direction! To master this trick, you'll have to practice, as though you're learning to write for the first time all over again.

**1** Cut out a 14-by-14-inch (35.5-by-35.5-cm) square of posterboard. Then curve its edges upward into a half-pipe with a 9-inch (23-cm) diameter.

**2** Find Mylar sheeting at a craft-supply store. Curve this "mirror" lengthwise to form a half-cylinder, then tape it smoothly on the inside of your posterboard half-pipe. Ta-da—you've got a *concave* mirror: A reflective surface that curves inward. (If you were to tape Mylar to the back of the half-pipe, you'd have a *convex* mirror.)

**3** Hold the mirror upright about 1 foot (30 cm) in front of you. Test it: Wink your right eye. Does your reflection in the mirror wink its right eye back? If not, move the mirror farther out until it does. This change occurs when you are beyond the mirror's *focal point*, the spot where light rays bouncing from the mirror meet. When you're very close to the curved mirror, however, it functions more like a flat mirror—much like the Earth looks flat because we're on it!

**4** Next, hold the mirror horizontally. Do you see your image turn upside down?

## What's the Deal?

When you peer into a flat mirror, the face that looks back is different from the one everyone else sees—it's flipped so that your left side is on the right, and vice versa. To explore this phenomenon, grab a piece of string and hold one end up to your right ear, then extend the other end to the right ear you see in the flat mirror. Notice how this ear is actually on the left side of the mirror? But when you try the same experiment with the half-pipe-shaped mirror, the light from your right ear bounces off the curved mirror and enters your eyes from the left—unflipping your face!

## Try This Next!

If you pay attention, you'll find reflective surfaces of all kinds all around you. Go on a mirror scavenger hunt around your home or neighborhood to see what objects reflect back an image of your own mug. Take, for instance, the spoon you eat your breakfast with in the morning. When you look at it with the bowl side up, it's a concave mirror; when you flip it over to see its shiny back, it's convex. What other secret mirrors can you find? What kind of mirrors are they?

# Unflip Your Face!

Your face in a mirror isn't really your face. Turn yourself around with this half-pipe mirror.

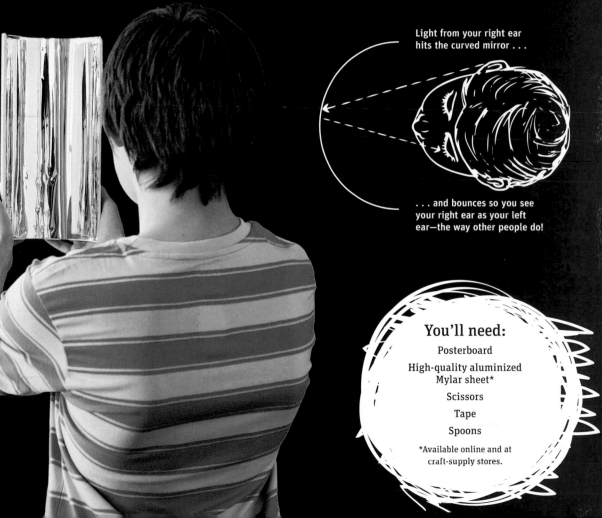

Light from your right ear hits the curved mirror . . .

. . . and bounces so you see your right ear as your left ear—the way other people do!

**You'll need:**

Posterboard

High-quality aluminized Mylar sheet*

Scissors

Tape

Spoons

*Available online and at craft-supply stores.

# Wander an Amazing Funhouse of Mirrors

Make your own distorted, crazy-wavy mirror to study angles of light.

**1** Ask your grown up to help remove two identical mirrors from their frames. Trace one frame onto the cardboard, but add 6 inches (15 cm) to its overall length. Repeat so that you have two tracings, then cut them both out.

**2** Cut several pieces of tracing paper to cover one opening of the box and fasten it there with tape.

**3** Cut the Mylar into two pieces the same size as the cardboard. Apply spray adhesive to the smooth side of both cardboard pieces, and apply the Mylar; trim any excess film around the board.

**4** Repeat with the other piece of mounted Mylar, but place the cardboard so that it curves inward from the frame.

## You'll need:

A grown up to help

Two identical mirror frames

Stiff piece of cardboard or posterboard at least as wide as and 6 inches (15 cm) longer than your mirror frames

Pencil

Scissors

Two pieces of high-quality Mylar sheeting at least as wide as and 6 inches (15 cm) longer than your mirror frames

Spray adhesive

Hot-glue gun

## What's the Deal?

Mirrors obey one main rule: The *angle of incidence*, at which light hits the mirror, equals the *angle of reflection*, at which light bounces off the mirror. Dividing these angles, perpendicular to the mirror, is the "normal" line—all angles are measured from the normal. In a flat mirror (such as in the diagram below), the angle of incidence is zero, meaning the light from your eyes bounces off the mirror and comes back at you along the perpendicular normal line. So when we're looking at curved mirrors, they either make us look taller because we have to look up for our line of sight to be normal to the mirror (as with concave mirrors), or shorter because we have to look down (as with convex ones).

**5** Stand the mirrors up against a wall. Experiment with the reflections by standing up close or far away, and with the mirror leaning against the wall at different angles. How do these angles change your reflection?

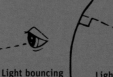

Light bouncing up to your eye from a convex mirror

Light bouncing down to your eye from a concave mirror

Light bouncing straight to your eye from a regular flat mirror

# Catch Light in a Box

Create tubular light patterns
with a box of mirrors.

**You'll need:**

Small cardboard box

Scissors

Mylar sheeting

Tracing paper

Tape

Clear plastic wrap

Various light sources, such as
fluorescent lights, incandescent
bulbs, computer or TV screens,
or colored lights

1. **Cut the flaps** off the cardboard box so that it's a frame with a window. Then trim down its depth so that it's fairly shallow, keeping in mind that each Mylar tube will need to be as long as your box is deep. Have plenty of Mylar on hand to roll enough tubes to fill up your box's shape.

2. **Cut several pieces** of tracing paper to cover one opening of the box and fasten it there with tape.

3. **Position your box** on a table with the open side facing up and cut pieces of Mylar as long as the box is deep.

4. **Roll the Mylar pieces** into tubes of different diameters, securing them with tape. (You can also experiment with the teardrop shapes you see to the left.) Fill the box with the tubes until they fit snugly.

5. **Trim the tops** of the tubes to just below the top of the box, then cover the box's open top with clear plastic wrap and tape the plastic in place.

6. **Go in search** of light sources. Hold your box so that the side covered with the frosted tracing paper is closest to you. Lift it to the light at different angles and distances, and check out the light patterns that move through the tubes.

*What's the Deal?*
The mirrored Mylar tubes are acting as light reflectors, bouncing patterns of colored light with beautiful intensity. By changing the angle of the box, thus changing the angles of incidence and reflection of light hitting the Mylar mirrors, you can change those patterns. The box is both an exploration tool and a piece of art itself.

Tape

Mylar tubes

Cardboard box

**1** Print the template with the circular grid of squares, which you can download at www.exploratorium.edu/exploring-light. Filling each box with only one or two colors, draw a simple picture—such as a house or smiley face.

**2** Take a look at your *anamorphic,* or distorted, grid: It has the same number and arrangement of spaces as your square grid, but the anamorphic grid's spaces have been stretched.

**3** Refer to the first box on your grid of squares, then count up to the corresponding block across the boundary where the two grids touch. Color in that block with the design that appears in the square, but flip it so it is upside down. Start at the boundary and work your way outward. Be patient and go slowly!

**4** When you're done coloring the grid, take your cylindrical mirror (or wrap Mylar around a soda can) and place it in the middle of the grid so that it covers the grid of squares.

**5** Check out the reflection in the mirror—can you see your original picture reflected back to you?

## What's the Deal?

You drew the same picture in your square and anamorphic grids, but in the anamorphic one, it was all stretched out and flipped. Yet mysteriously, the distorted shape that you see reflected in the cylindrical mirror looked like your original drawing. How come? You've already learned that the angle at which light hits a mirror (called the *angle of incidence*) is equal to the angle at which the light bounces off the mirror (its *angle of reflection*). So your image's vertical lines are only slightly curved in the anamorphic grid, but your sideways lines have to curve a lot in order to undo the distortion and appear straight in the mirror's reflection. The result is a mind-blowing masterpiece!

Compose your picture on the square grid using simple color blocks . . .

. . . then transfer each colored block to the opposite space on the anamorphic grid. Flip your drawing like you see here!

# Transform Your Art with a Mystery Mirror

Make amazing anamorphic art out of just two grids and a mirror.

### You'll need:

Printer and paper

Anamorphic grid download from www.exploratorium.edu/exploring-light

Colored pencils or markers

A cylindrical mirror, or high-quality Mylar sheeting wrapped around a soda can

# Green

Green is the color of life, occupying the visible spectrum between 520 and 570 nanometers. We identify its vibrant hues with nature, freshness, and hope, and we've evolved to see it quite well, given its prime spot in the middle of the visible spectrum. Green may be common, but it still pops up in some surprising places . . .

At sunset, Earth's atmosphere acts like a prism, separating the image of the Sun into different colors, with red at the bottom, followed by orange and yellow, and violet at the top. As the Sun sets, the red, orange, and yellow disappear first, leaving only green, blue, and violet. But our atmosphere scatters the violet and blue from the sunlight, so we very rarely see them. Instead, if it's a notably clear day, we may glimpse a quick emerald green at the edge of the Sun before it disappears.

Green
flash

Green
stars

Many animals try to escape the watchful eyes of predators by blending into their surroundings. Since so much of nature is green, it's ended up the camouflage color of choice for many frogs, lizards, and insects.

Hey, why are there no green stars? All stars actually emit a wide range of colors, and a star that emits most of its light as green also happens to emit large amounts of red and blue light. This combination of red, green, and blue light appears white to a human eye. (The photo here is actually of a green cloud of cosmic gas, which only emits green light. That's why it looks green to us!)

Camouflage

Chlorophyll makes plants and algae appear green, but this chemical also serves an important role in *photosynthesis,* the process by which plants convert sunlight to energy. Chlorophyll molecules absorb light in the blue and red parts of the visible spectrum for use as plant fuel.

Night vision

Chlorophyll

Night-vision goggles work by either amplifying trace amounts of light in near darkness, or using thermal-imaging technology to pick up on the infrared light that objects emit. Both methods include phosphor, a chemical that radiates green light, in order to take advantage of the fact that the rod cells in our eyes see green the best in low-light conditions.

Green patina

A patina is to copper what rust is to iron: A color effect produced by oxidation. So when copper is exposed to rain, salt, acid rain, and carbon dioxide, the sulfur, oxygen, and chlorine react with the metal's surface to produce copper sulfate and copper chloride, which appear blue-green. You can see this effect on outdoor copper statues or old pennies!

## Try This Next!

Get your hands on some glow-in-the-dark stars—the kind you might stick on your ceiling for an eternally starry night. Soak some in hot water and some in cold water, then try shining a light on them to charge them up. Which stars glow more brightly and which glow longer? Why do you think this is? (Hint: Higher temperatures cause molecules to move faster. When they bump into each other, they release stored energy as light.)

1. **Paint your foam board** with several coats of phosphorescent paint and let it dry, then lean it against a wall. Turn off any overhead lights.

2. **Hold your hand** between the glow board and a regular flashlight. Flash the light on for a moment, then quickly off. You caught your shadow! How long does it stick around?

3. **Take one of your colored flashlights** (keeping overhead lights off), turn it on, hold it around 2 inches (5 cm) away from the glow board, and move it around—try writing your name or drawing a simple picture. (But don't actually touch the glow board—you'll scratch it.)

4. **Repeat with all** the colors. Which make the clearest, brightest light paintings on the glow board? How long does it take for them to fade?

## What's the Deal?

When light hits the phosphorescent paint, electrons absorb the light's energy and get energized. When they calm down, light is emitted, producing a nifty green glow on any area of the board that wasn't covered by your jumping, cartwheeling, or twirling shadow. The colored lights affected it differently because of their varying energy levels. Since blue and UV light have the highest energies, they excite the most electrons in the paint, thus making the most light—and creating longer-lasting, sharp shadows of you doing your thing!

# Trap Your Shadow with Phosphorescence

Strike a pose and see it last on a green, glowing backdrop.

**You'll need:**

Large piece of foam board

Phosphorescent paint*

Paintbrush

A darkened room

Flashlights, regular and colored**

Glow-in-the-dark stars

Hot and cold water

*Available at craft-supply stores and online.

**The light from a camera phone works well, too!

Laser beams mysteriously bend when they pass through different substances—why?

# Bend a Saber of Laser Light!

**1** Let's start by observing a basic laser bend. (Named from an acronym that stands for "Light Amplification by Stimulated Emission of Radiation," lasers are powerful light sources, so absolutely *no* aiming them at your or others' eyes.) Fill a glass with water, then stir in a teeny dash of milk—this will allow you to see the laser light as it passes through the glass.

**2** Kill the lights and point the laser through the side of the glass, observing it from above. Do you see how the beam bends when it hits the glass and passes through the water?

**3** Now try aiming the laser from near the bottom of the glass up to the water's surface. Does the laser beam pass through the water, or does it bounce back down to the bottom?

**You'll need:**
A laser pointer with less than 1 mW output (for safety)
Clear glass or fishbowl
Water
Milk
A darkened room
Several small mirrors
Clean, clear plastic bottle, 1 L or bigger
Nail or Phillips screwdriver
Cornstarch
Microscope slide

**4** Grab a few small mirrors. Play with placing them inside the glass where the laser beam hits, and watch the light ricochet like a ball bouncing off the pavement!

Turn the page ⟹

## What's the Deal?

We've already learned that light moves in straight lines—and even in these experiments, it still does, but it changes direction when moving between water and air. This is because light moves at different speeds through these two substances, making the path of light bend when the water exits the bottle. This phenomenon is called *refraction*. When you saw water stream through the hole in your plastic bottle, you observed it in *laminar flow*, moving in a smooth and uninterrupted current that's ideal for carrying light. When the beam hit the stream as it exited the bottle, its light was trapped and reflected inside the water in a phenomenon called *total internal reflection*. In this way, the stream acted like a fiber optic cable, carrying the light along its arc.

**5** **Next, grab a clear plastic bottle.** Poke a small circular hole in its side with a nail. (A grown up can use a Phillips screwdriver, which makes a more precise hole.) Set the bottle over a sink, then fill it with water and a tiny bit of milk. Put the cap on.

**6** **Hold the laser** on the side of the bottle opposite the hole, then turn it on so its beam projects horizontally toward the hole. (Use something to prop it up!)

**7** **Darken the room** again and clap cornstarch in the air so that the beam is visible. Take off the bottle's cap and lo and behold—water arcs out of the bottle, and the laser light bends to follow the water's stream!

### Try This Next!

Line up a few mirrors so that they're parallel to each other. (It helps to prop them up, as we've done here with paper clips and tape.) Clap a little cornstarch in the air, then shine the laser beam between mirrors. Adjust the angle of incidence very carefully until you "trap" the beam between the mirrors, bouncing it back and forth in a dazzling accordion pattern. Still haven't had enough? Set a microscope slide at 45 degrees to a laser's beam and (after more cornstarch clapping) turn the laser on. When the beam hits the transparent but reflective slide, part of the beam will pass through, but another part will reflect back! This is called a *beam splitter*.

# Phenomenal Polarized Phun

## Use filters to block light—or make a stained-glass window without glass!

When the polarizing filters are oriented in the same direction, both let light pass through them.

When one polarizing filter is rotated, it absorbs (or blocks) the light.

## What's the Deal?

Light is vibration. It travels in waves that wiggle in all directions. But a *polarizing filter* only transmits light that vibrates in one specific direction—for example, up and down, or left and right. So when you look through the aligned filters, light shines through both. When you rotate one to make them perpendicular to each other, however, no light gets through because the first polarizer only transmits, say, up-and-down vibrating light, while the second only transmits left-and-right vibrating light, blocking all the up-and-down light. When you add tape, its long, stretchy molecules twist the light in new directions, but only colors aligned with the second filter get through. The result? A kaleidoscopic play of colors as you rotate each sheet!

**1** Buy polarizing filter sheets. Found in sunglasses and camera lenses, these inexpensive sheets filter light, cut down on glare and reflections, and enhance colors.

**2** Stack the filters one on top of the other and hold them up to a window. Rotate one of the filters—see how the light goes darker the more you rotate the filters?

**3** Explore transparencies. Stick bits of Scotch packing tape in crisscross patterns on both sheets. Overlap some strips or form words or pictures. Then put the sheets together with the tape in between them in a "sandwich."

**4** Hold the sheets up to a window's light. Rotate them in opposite directions. Gorgeous colors and geometric shapes appear and disappear, and the words and pictures slide in and out of view.

## What's the Deal?

The lens you hold in your hands is a *Fresnel lens*. Its surface is made up of many concentric circles (like the rings on a tree), with each ring more sloped the closer it is to the magnifier's edge. We call this magnifier a *positive* (or *converging*) lens because it bends parallel light rays as they pass perpendicularly through the lens's grooves, making the rays meet at the *focal point* and creating a magnified image. (In this case, that of your friend's face behind the lens!) Page magnifiers have a *focal length*—the distance between the lens's center and its focal point—of about 10 inches (25 cm), which is likely right where your friend started looking her sharpest!

① **First, run your fingers** over your page magnifier's seemingly flat surface. Feel the tiny ridges on one side? Do you note any changes in the ridges' elevation? Are they arranged in a shape?

② **Now stand facing a friend** and extend one of your arms out straight in front of you. Have your friend hold an arm out, too, so that your hands meet.

③ **Ask your friend** to hold the page magnifier with her other hand near her face (goofy smiles strongly encouraged), then slowly move it toward you.

④ **Now it's your turn.** Grab the page magnifier and bring it to your face until it touches your nose. How does your friend's face look to you as you do this? And how does your face look to your friend?

## Try This Next!

To observe Fresnel lenses in the wild, go no farther than your nearest lighthouse! The lens gets its name from French physicist Augustin-Jean Fresnel, who developed it specifically for lighthouses. A Fresnel lens in a lighthouse captures the light from the lamp and focuses it into a narrow parallel beam, making it visible at great distances for sailors. The Fresnel lens in this activity features a large aperture (an adjustable opening that controls the amount of light that passes through it) and short focal length, which require less mass and volume than a conventional lens—so it can be manufactured in a flat, lightweight sheet.

# Bend Light (and Your Mind!) Through a Lens

## Fresnel lenses make your friends look more interesting.

A Fresnel lens, viewed from the side. The tiny, concentric grooves help to bend and focus light.

### You'll need:
Large Fresnel page magnifier*

A friend

*Available for cheap at online education-supply stores. Just be careful where you store it: These can cause fires if left in direct sunlight.

Tiny optics tools are
hiding all around you.

# Surprising
# Lenses

1. **On a rainy day,** find a ground-floor window and peer at the raindrops clinging to the glass outside—they're curved outward (*convex*), just like a lens in a magnifying glass. Study what you see through the drop. The world now looks upside down, and bigger!

2. **Put on your rain boots** and get outside. Peek through the same window's droplets. The entire room is still flipped upside down.

3. **Head back inside** and spread a newspaper on a table. Place a clear plastic lid on top of the paper, then flick a few water drops onto the lid.

4. **Peer through the drops** at the paper. Can you read the words? Now slowly lift up the lid. What happens to the words?

## What's the Deal?

All lenses bend light to magnify or shrink what we see. But lenses needn't be glass or plastic. Ice, apple juice, Jello—any clear substance can work as a lens. When light rays pass through a lens, they either *converge* (come together) or *diverge* (spread out), depending on the lens shape. When you looked through a raindrop, it naturally acted as a convex lens, converging rays and inverting the view both outside and inside your window. Convex lenses also magnify—which is why you had an easier time reading the newspaper through the drops!

Convex lens

Subject

Flipped image

Clever manipulation of light can create
a camera the size of a whole room.

# Hang Out in a Giant Camera Obscura

## You'll need:

Room with a window
Black posterboard or black trash bags
Black gaffer tape
Craft knife
Ruler
White sheet
Camera with a long exposure setting
Cardboard tube
Aluminum foil
Waxed paper
Tape
Black construction paper

1. **Choose a window** that will become your *aperture*—an opening that light passes through. It's best if outside that window, you can see (or create!) a scene that will make for an interesting picture.

2. **Using black posterboard** or trash bags and black gaffer tape, completely cover any windows that aren't the one you'll be using as your view to the world. Save one bag or piece of posterboard and carefully cut out a small hole ¼ inch (6.4 mm) in diameter with the craft knife.

3. **Secure the posterboard** over the window to black it out. Turn off the lights in the room and check for any sneaky light cracks (such as under doors or around the sides of the posterboard), then cover them up. If the wall opposite your aperture is not blank, hang a white sheet over it to create a screen.

4. **Now turn off the lights!** Let your eyes adjust for a full minute, then check out your projected image. If you have a camera with a long exposure setting, set it to at least 30 seconds and document the outside captured on the inside.

## What's the Deal?

The *camera obscura* (literally, "dark room") illustrates the physics of any camera: The image outside passes through a hole and is projected upside down on the opposite surface. But why does it flip? Outside the hole, lots of light rays are reflecting in all directions. Each travels in a straight line, but they start at different places. A light ray that comes from on high (say, from the sky in this image) will pass through the hole and project clouds on the floor. But a light ray from down low (one coming from the sea) will travel to the ceiling, bringing its ocean view with it. Each ray in between the high and low rays adds its own two cents until the upside-down picture is complete.

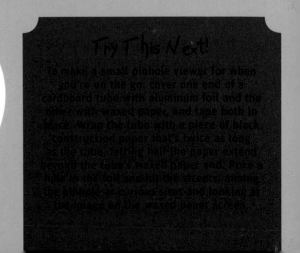

### Try This Next!

To make a small pinhole viewer for when you're on the go, cover one end of a cardboard tube with aluminum foil and the other with waxed paper, and tape both in place. Wrap the tube with a piece of black construction paper that's twice as long as the tube, letting half the paper extend beyond the taped waxed paper end. Poke a hole in the foil and hit the streets, aiming the pinhole at curious sites and looking at the image on the waxed paper screen.

# Blue

Surveys have found that people really, really like blue. No surprise why: Some of the most peaceful, refreshing things are blue—such as the sky on a clear day, or the waves at the beach. Falling between 450 and 495 nanometers, blue has one of the shortest wavelengths, which makes it ideal for scattering throughout our atmosphere and spreading pleasantly all around.

Alpha male mandrills boast vivid blue ridged noses, which signal to potential mates that they're prime parenting material. Curiously, a mandrill's over-the-top colors fade if his status is threatened, but he can get hi bright marks back if he flexes some muscle in his clan.

Male
mandri

Underwater

Believe it or not, no one has blue pigment in their eye. Eyes appear blue because wavelengths in white light g "scattered" by large molecules in the iris, while the re of white light's colors get absorbed by the dark tissue the back of the iris.

Blue
eyes

Next time you go for a dip, check out the colors around you. Objects near the surface that are a vivid red—your swim trunks, perhaps!—take on an aqua tint. That's because light's full spectrum can't penetrate deep into the water. Longer light waves (such as red) are absorbed first, then each color disappears—orange, yellow, green, and so on—the deeper you go. By 300 feet (91 m), blue disappears, too.

When a snowflake first falls on a glacier, it has many reflective surfaces. But over hundreds of years, the snowflakes get compressed, squeezing out air bubbles and leaving no facets for light to bounce off. Instead, the red end of light's spectrum is absorbed by the ice, transmitting an electric blue back to you.

Robin's eggs

The distinct turquoise of robin's eggs is a mystery. One hunch is that blue eggs evolved because they blend in with the sky, making them invisible to predators on the ground looking up through holes in nests. We do know, however, that birds create their own unique egg colors in their pigmentation glands. This probably helps them know whose egg is whose!

Glacial blue

Blue flame

If you've ever watched a candle or a lit burner on your stove, you've likely noticed a peek-a-boo blue near the center of the flame. Surprisingly, this part of the blaze is the hottest at 2,552°F (1,400°C). The flame goes from blue to yellow to orange, then to red at a merely balmy 1,472°F (800°C).

1. **Go on a tour of your home,** scouting for objects to expose on your sunprint paper. Remember that the Sun will capture an object's overall shape but not its texture or details.

2. **In a dark place,** far away from the Sun's rays, place a sheet of the sunprint paper on your movable work surface with its blue side facing up, and lay your objects on the paper. Note that when you move the tray into direct sunlight, the light will develop any areas of the paper that aren't covered, so position your objects in a way that will show off their shapes.

3. **Now for the crucial moment.** Move your surface outside to a spot that gets lots of direct sunshine. Watch the blue paper turn whitish in about one to five minutes—your sunprint has been exposed!

4. **Move everything back indoors** and remove your objects. Rinse your sunprint in cold water and let it dry on paper towels.

5. **Watch your sunprint** as the image emerges. To press, place heavy books on top once it's dry.

## What's the Deal?

Sunprint paper has been treated with a solution of potassium ferricyanide and ferric ammonium citrate. This iron solution is photosensitive, meaning that if you expose it to light, it will undergo a chemical change. When you laid your paper out in the Sun with objects on top of it, the space around your objects and their shadows was changed by the light, while the area below the objects was shielded, creating the silhouette images. The chemical solution on the paper reacted with the water when you rinsed it, yielding the final product.

## Try This Next!

With a little patience, you can skip the photosensitive paper and make images with the Sun using stuff that's lying around your house. Try layering pieces of plain old construction paper and leaving them in a window for a few days—or arranging scrap wood on your lawn—to see how the Sun fades the negative space in your design.

# Make Sunprints

## All you need to take these wondrous images is a bright day and cyanotype paper.

### You'll need:

Objects with strong silhouettes—flowers, slinkies, jewelry, tools, and toys

Sunprint (also called cyanotype) paper*

A darkened room

A movable work surface such as a tray

Lots of sunlight

Cold water

Cloth or paper towels

Books or other heavy objects

Construction paper

Scrap wood

Your lawn

*Available online or at science or craft-supply stores.

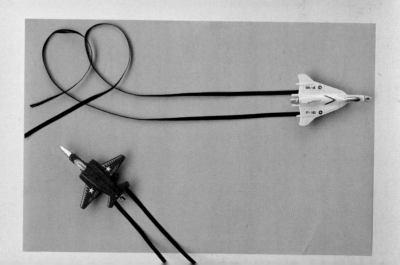

With a little help from a solar panel, you can make art with the Sun.

# Solar-Powered Scribbling Machine

**1** **First, you need** to connect a DC motor to the solar panel. To do so, first look on the solar panel and find the "+" and "−" marks, then locate the terminal where the wires connect to the motor.

**2** **Strip the ends** of two wires—about ¼ inch (6.4 mm). Twist one wire to the solar panel's positive terminal and the other to its negative terminal, then attach both wires to the motor's terminals with alligator clips. We sometimes find that machines work best with two solar panels, so experiment with wiring two solar panels together for more juice.

**3** **Scrounge up a base**—an item that's light enough that the motor can propel it, but big enough to fit the motor and solar panel. Strawberry baskets, cardboard-box lids, egg cartons—all are fun options to explore.

**4** **Now take a look** at your motor. See the tip that protrudes? When the motor is connected to power, that tip spins, propelling your scribbler. So when you attach the motor to your base, this crucial bit still needs to be able to rotate, and it needs something on its end with some weight to create more force. Experiment with attaching glue sticks, pencil stubs, or other items to this tip so that they're offset and can rotate freely.

**5** **Attach your motor** and solar panel to the base with masking tape. Position the motor so that the glue stick or other object can spin.

**6** **Next, figure out** how to affix your chalk pieces to your base. Try attaching them to the base as legs so that they "walk," or use a pipe cleaner or wire to extend the chalk so that it drags on the ground as the machine moves. You may need to wrap the chalk in foam or plastic to secure it to the base. Tinker until you find a method that creates a neat pattern of chalk!

**7** **Put your solar** panel in the sunlight to test. To change the intensity, cover part of the solar panel using mirrors or lenses.

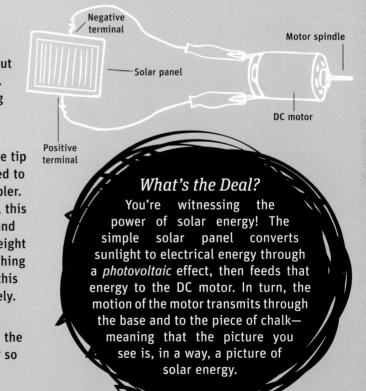

Negative terminal

Motor spindle

Solar panel

Positive terminal

DC motor

### What's the Deal?
You're witnessing the power of solar energy! The simple solar panel converts sunlight to electrical energy through a *photovoltaic* effect, then feeds that energy to the DC motor. In turn, the motion of the motor transmits through the base and to the piece of chalk—meaning that the picture you see is, in a way, a picture of solar energy.

# Rainbow in a Bottle

Build a mud terrarium, then watch bacteria move in and make it their own colorful home!

1. **Go get some mud!** Visit the banks of a local lake, creek, or pond and gather buckets of good and gooey dirt. (Extra credit: Go to a few different mud sources so you can start separate containers and compare and contrast results.)

2. **Pick out rocks** and stir water into the separate mud types until they're the consistency of heavy cream or a mud milkshake (yum!).

3. **Mix shredded newspaper** and an egg into your different mud types, then pour them into separate clear containers, making sure to leave about 1 inch (2.5 cm) at the top of each one.

4. **Top off the mud** with a drizzle of water. Seal the containers with plastic wrap and a rubber band.

5. **Place the mud columns** in a sunny spot. Every few days, open the plastic wrap to vent the gases and add more water if needed.

6. **In six to eight weeks,** you'll see bacteria in brilliant colors. Note where which colors appear and how they change over time.

## What's the Deal?

The rainbows that you see are colonies of billions of bacteria. Some are decomposers that feed on organic matter, such as the carbon in the newspaper and the sulfur in the egg. Eventually, they'll eat up all the oxygen near the container's bottom and give off carbon dioxide. This is mighty tasty for the mud's green photosynthetic bacteria, who use light, carbon, and hydrogen to make carbohydrates and emit oxygen. Then there are the red, orange, and green bacteria near the bottom that are photosynthetic but oxygen-intolerant, so they get their hydrogen from hydrogen sulfide, released when the decomposers break down the egg. Your mud terrarium hosted all these bacteria to begin with—you just gave them ideal conditions to thrive, reproduce, and create symbiotic relationships with one another.

# Indigo

Technically, indigo is only on the spectrum because Sir Isaac Newton put it there, assuming there would be seven shades as there are seven notes on a musical scale. Physicists now think its inclusion is iffy (they can't even agree if it falls between 420 and 450 or 446 and 464 nanometers), but everyone can agree that it's beautiful.

One of the most familiar uses of indigo is in the denim that may be on your legs right now. Denim fades as it's worn, particularly at sites of stress (such as your knees) creating patterns of fading unique to the owner. Denim also crocks, meaning its blue dye rubs off on your skin!

Denim

Scientists use color to help them see what is invisible to the unaided eye. For example, at crime scenes, luminol glows blue when it comes into contact with the iron found in even the most minute amounts of blood. It helps detectives track bad guys—even if they clean up!

Indigofera tinctoria

Famous and sought-after for many centuries, *Indigofera tinctoria* is the original source of indigo dye in nature. To get dark-blue pigment from this shrub, its leaves undergo a good soak in water and then are left to ferment. The resulting substance gets mixed with a base (such as lye), compressed into cakes, and dried into a deep blue powder.

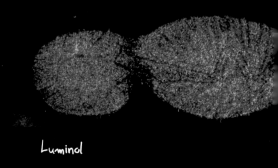

Luminol

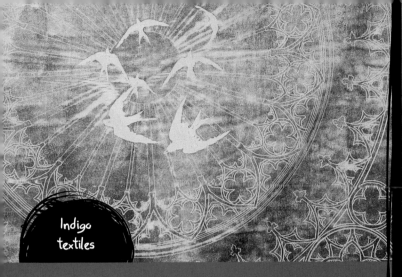

The indigo bunting gets its name from its shimmery indigo color. But there's no blue pigment in its feathers! Instead, the color is created by a pattern of keratin (the same protein that makes up our skin, hair, and nails), which reflects a jewel-tone blue and allows the yellow in white light to be absorbed. Hold a blue feather up with the light behind it to glimpse its true color: A dark, dull brown.

Indigo bunting

Once you've got a nice big batch of indigo dye, how does this chalky blue stuff get into your clothes? The powder gets stirred into a mix of water, salt, soda ash, and sodium hydroxide until it starts to turn a surprising pea green. This mix then either becomes a soaking bath for a cotton garment, or it's rolled onto a carved woodblock for use in textiles. Once the colored item gets exposed to air, the dye reacts with oxygen and turns indigo.

Lactarius indigo

Imagine if you saw one of these peculiar mushrooms while on a stroll through the forest! Commonly known as the indigo milk cap mushroom, this unique fungus grows all over North America, East Asia, and Central America. Cut one open and you'll see a trickle of bright blue ooze (or latex), but not for long: It dries green the longer it's exposed to air.

# Catch Rainbows with a CD

**A simple compact disc makes crazy colorful patterns.**

You'll need:

Sunshine

Piece of posterboard or
wall in the shade

Several CDs

Craft paper

Scissors

1. **Head outside** on a bright day or find an especially sunny spot inside your house. Station yourself so that the posterboard is in the shade but the CD is in direct sunlight. Point the silver mirrored side of the CD at the posterboard, angled so it reflects sunlight onto the surface. (If you don't have posterboard, a wall can work, too, as long as it is in shadow.)

2. **Adjust the posterboard** and the CD until a circular reflection of bright light appears on the white surface. Look around this ring of light for circular bands of color, then experiment with the distance of the CD from the posterboard to create the most vivid colors possible.

3. **Next, hold your CD** between your thumb and middle finger and try bending the disc in and out. Watch the posterboard to see how changing the shape of the disc affects the light's reflection and the spray of rainbows.

4. **Once you've unleashed** these colors, get inventive with the shapes that you make! Try folding a piece of paper in half, cutting it into a circular disc, and then cutting a pattern into the folded disc. Unfold the paper circle, tape it over the CD's mirrored side, and point it at the posterboard again. The paper will obstruct some light rays from the CD but let others sneak through, creating wowing patterns of color and light.

## What's the Deal?

You've already learned that a CD is an example of a *diffraction grating,* a tool that separates light into distinct colors of the rainbow. That's because a CD's surface has a tightly packed spiral groove. Its fine, regular spacing bends each color of light at a slightly different angle, making that color visible to our eyes. Note how, in your rainbow circles, blue is the inside ring. Why is this? Blue has the smallest wavelength of any color in the visible spectrum, and so is diffracted at the smallest angle. The shapes and circles of light you see are called *caustics,* and they occur when light shines through or reflects off a curved surface.

# The Glow Show

Crack open a glow stick to learn about chemiluminescence.

**You'll need:**

2 sturdy glasses
Ice water and hot water
Glow sticks
A grown up to help
Protective gloves
Protective eyewear
Kitchen scissors
2 or more clear plastic cups
Dishtowel
Highlighter marker
Paintbrush
Black light

**1** Fill two glasses: one with ice water and one with hot water. Crack two fresh glow sticks and put one in each glass. Crack a third and leave it out. What happens to their brightness? How long does this change take?

**2** After a few minutes, switch the sticks and watch them do their thing. Which ones go dim? Which ones glow more? Are these fast or slow transformations?

**3** The next part of this activity is super cool, but it has to be done by an adult wearing protective gloves and goggles. Instruct your helper to cut off the tip of a new glow stick with scissors, then pour its liquid into a cup.

**4** Check out the cartridge—you'll note a glass capsule with liquid in it. Your grown up should remove this capsule, wrap it in a dish cloth, and gently break it open. This liquid goes into a second plastic cup.

**5** Dim the lights and pour the solution back and forth several times to mix it. The potion should begin to glow before your eyes. You've just re-created the chemical reaction that happens inside a glow stick when you crack and shake it at parties!

## Try This Next!

With the help of an adult, put on some gloves and open up a highlighter marker—an adult may need to saw it open. Take out the pigment cartridge inside and squeeze it into a glass of water, then let the cartridge soak in the water. Once all the pigment has been released, take a paintbrush, dip it in the highlighter juice, and paint a tattoo on your arm. Check it out under a black light! This is an example of fluorescence.

## What's the Deal?

The key word here is *chemilumin-escence*: When certain chemicals are mixed, they can undergo a chemical reaction and produce light. When you crack a glow stick, a capsule of hydrogen peroxide breaks, mixing with a surrounding solution of phenyl oxalate ester and fluorescent dye. This mix creates a way-cool chemiluminescent reaction. As you saw, heat increases the rate of the reaction and makes the glow stick bright for a little while, but cold slows the reaction and makes make it dim longer. If you ever want to save a glow stick, put it in the freezer!

# Paint with Light!

Light up the night with amazing art using a nifty long-exposure method.

**1** **Scrounge up light sources!** The standard flashlight from the kitchen junk drawer works great, but there are also pen lights, bike lights, glow sticks, electroluminescent (EL) wire, holiday lights, and sparklers—even toys with flashing lights and cell-phone screens will make a cool look. You can also tape an LED's long leg to the positive side of a 3-volt watch battery.

**2** **Set up the camera** in a darkened room (though it may be easier to set up when the lights are still on). It's helpful to have a tripod so that your camera stays steady during all the action. If you don't have one, try improvising with a table and a stack of books. Have your friend get behind the camera while you stand in front, holding whatever light sources you've collected.

**3** **Set your camera** to take long-exposure photos (10 seconds or longer). This function may be labeled "Shutter Priority" or "Bulb" on your camera.

**4** **Turn out the lights,** have your friend press the camera's shutter release button, and make a "painting" with the light source—try writing your name! Your friend can tell you when to start and stop so that your entire masterpiece is in the photo; pause to check that your entire image appears in the frame.

Turn the page ⟹

Watch battery

LED

98

**5** **Try a new light source.** What effect does a blinking bike light have? What about a long tangle of EL wire? Or several LEDs tossed across the room? What happens if you use a flashlight with a different color, or tape a piece of colored acetate over your light's beam?

**6** **Tell a story** with your light painting. Have a friend stand still during the exposure while you draw, say, ears or a hat on him or her from behind, or complete a scene (such as an empty swing!) with a stick figure. If you can't see your friend in the picture, just shine a light on him or her for a few seconds!

### What's the deal?

Speaking generally, a camera produces an image by capturing the light coming from different sources inside its frame. When a flash or natural light source bathes a scene in light, the camera has an easy time capturing the full image lickety-split. But in low light, the camera needs more time to collect the info needed to create an image. A long shutter speed allows the camera to collect what your eye would see during the course of 10 to 30 seconds and shows it to you all at once, making the image appear as though it has been "painted" as a static, continuous image. So why doesn't everything look like a light painting to our eyes? Because the brain and retina "refresh" between 25 and 40 times per second, clearing out old images to make room for new ones.

# Power Up LEDs

Do colored LEDs eat up different amounts of energy? Rig this circuit to see!

**You'll need:**

Red, green, and blue LEDs—more colors, if you can find them*

200 ohm resistors, one for each LED*

1 kohm potentiometer*

2 AA batteries*

Battery holder*

2 uncoated jumbo paper clips

Clear tape

Hole punch

Large piece of cardboard for a tray

Insulated wire

*Available online or at hobbyist stores.

**1** **Pick up a few** crucial but cheap parts: *LEDs* (light-emitting diodes) in lots of colors, *resistors* (electronic components that reduce current flow within a circuit), a *potentiometer* (a device that allows you to vary the power in a circuit), two AA batteries, and a battery holder.

**2** **Connect each LED** to a resistor by twisting the LED's short end with one of the resistors' ends. To do this, make an X with the two pieces of insulated wire, twist it twice, fold the ends into a V shape, and twist it again on both sides.

**3** **Weave each LED's longer leg** through a paper clip. Then use the same technique to fasten all the free resistor ends to a second paper clip. Secure all the ends with tape, leaving enough paper clip exposed to attach one more wire.

**4** **The potentiometer** has a nut that screws onto its dial. With your hole punch, make a hole in the cardboard, then stick the dial through it. Screw the nut onto the dial.

**5** **Tape all your components** onto the cardboard. Using a piece of insulated wire, connect the middle terminal of the potentiometer to the paper clip attached to the LEDs. Then connect the first terminal of the potentiometer to the paper clip attached to the resistors using another piece of insulated wire.

**6** **Attach the positive lead** from the battery to the potentiometer's third terminal. Attach the battery's negative lead to the paper clip attached to the resistor.

**7** **Finally, slowly turn the dial** of the potentiometer to add voltage, going from 0 up to 3 volts. Do the LEDs light up one at a time or in any particular order?

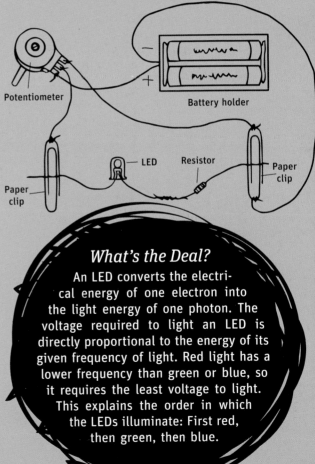

Potentiometer

Battery holder

LED    Resistor    Paper clip

Paper clip

### *What's the Deal?*
An LED converts the electrical energy of one electron into the light energy of one photon. The voltage required to light an LED is directly proportional to the energy of its given frequency of light. Red light has a lower frequency than green or blue, so it requires the least voltage to light. This explains the order in which the LEDs illuminate: First red, then green, then blue.

# Violet

Last in the lineup of colors on the visible spectrum, violet falls between 380 and 450 nanometers, meaning it has the shortest wavelength of them all. Vivid yet deep, violet pigments pop up throughout history and around the world as rare and highly valued. The color also shows up in nature as an interesting indicator of science at work.

The discovery of this pale purple is a lovely accident. In 1856, chemist Sir William Henry Perkin was trying to create an artificial form of quinine (to cure malaria), but made a beautiful purple residue by mistake. This became the first manufactured dye, also called Perkin's mauve.

Mauve

In scientific terms, *anthocyanins* are water-soluble pigments that appear blue, red, or purple, depending on their pH level (how acidic or basic they are). In food terms, anthocyanins are what give blueberries, cranberries, raspberries, blackberries, cherries, red cabbages, and eggplants their deep, cool hues.

Murex snail

This snail may seem like an ordinary sea snail—until you see the brilliant blue-violet dye made from its mucus. The use of this dye dates back to the ancient Phoenicians, who treated the dye as such a precious commodity that it was only used by the aristocracy—hence the term "royal blue."

Anthocyanins

Amethyst

A gray color as a solid, iodine deceivingly gets its name from the Greek *iodes*, meaning "violet." This Greek root alludes to one of iodine's awesomest properties: It can help produce purple haze! This distinctive purple smoke is produced when a scientist—and only a scientist!—carefully mixes aluminum, powdered iodine, and water.

Iodine vapor

If your birthday is in February, you're probably already familiar with the purple quartz known as amethyst. Amethyst geodes formed long ago when gas pockets expanded inside molten lava, which created cavities when the lava cooled. Then, silicon dioxide led to the formation of the crystals inside the cavities; their color is created by the presence iron.

UV vision

Violet is the last color on the visible spectrum that we humans can see, but it turns out that bees can detect ultraviolet light, which falls just beyond 400 nanometers. This ability allows them to detect patterns of UV coloration on flowers, which scientists call "landing strips": They help bees alight on areas that are rich in nectar and pollen, their food.

105

# Index

# Index

# Activity Credits

Thanks to all the Exploratorium staff and participants of the Teacher Institute, Tinkering Studio, Institute for Inquiry, Extended Learning, and Community Youth Programs who contributed to the creation, testing, and continued development of these activities. In particular, certain activities couldn't have happened without Richard O. Brown, Paul Doherty, Ken Finn, Ron Hipschman, Thomas Humphrey, Karen Kalumuck, Lori Lambertson, Eric Muller, Don Rathjen, Linda Shore, Modesto Tamez, and Julie Yu.

Special thanks to Taizo Matsumura for developing the Mylar lightbox activity on page 64.

# Weldon Owen Acknowledgments

Weldon Owen would like to thank the Exploratorium for blowing our minds with science throughout the creation of this book. Special thanks go to rock-star educators Paul Doherty, Ken Finn, Ron Hipschman, Eric Muller, Mike Petrich, Linda Shore, and Julie Yu for their invaluable help in evaluating the book's content. We'd also like to thank Julie Nunn, Silva Raker, Dana Goldberg, Amy Snyder, and Megan Bury for their enthusiasm, expertise, and assistance. The Exploratorium also gratefully acknowledges its Catalyst Circle Committee for its leadership in resource development, which advances the museum's educational mission.

We'd also like to express gratitude to our photo shoot team: our photograher, Katrine Naleid; Stephen Austin Welch; Victor Wong; stylist Pamela Campbell; assistant stylist Hilary Seeley; and studio teachers Carolyn Crimley, Bonnie Hughes, and Nancy Riordan. We'd also like to thank Elissa Worley at Exalt Models and all our amazing kid scientists on set: Annalie, Brian, Cruz, Emily, Faith, Gianna, Giovanni, Isabella, Jonathan, Kaylyn, Mariah, Matthew, Sydney, and Taylor.

We also must give a hearty thanks to Jacqueline Aaron, Kevin Broccoli, Emily Clark, Sarah Edelstein, Jan Hughes, Katharine Moore, and Marisa Solís for editorial assistance and Andreina Prado and Hilary Seeley for design help.

# weldon**owen**

**President, CEO** Terry Newell
**VP, Sales** Amy Kaneko
**VP, Publisher** Roger Shaw
**Director of Finance** Philip Paulick

**Senior Editor** Lucie Parker
**Project Editor** Laura Goode
**Editorial Assistant** Jaime Alfaro

**Creative Director** Kelly Booth
**Art Director** Lorraine Rath
**Project Art Director** Meghan Hildebrand
**Senior Production Designer** Rachel Lopez Metzger

**Production Director** Chris Hemesath
**Associate Production Director** Michelle Duggan

Weldon Owen is a division of **BONNIER**

Library of Congress Control Number: 2014944960

ISBN 13: 978-1-61628-799-3
ISBN 10: 1-61628-799-3

10 9 8 7 6 5 4 3 2 1
2014 2015 2016 2017 2018

Printed in China by RR Donnelley.

# expl○ratorium®

Pier 15, San Francisco, CA 94111
www.exploratorium.edu

The Exploratorium is San Francisco's renowned museum of
science, art, and human perception. The content in this book
began as exhibitions, workshops, and activities created through
the Exploratorium's educational and professional development
programs. These long-standing, highly regarded programs include
the Teacher Institute, which supports secondary science and math
teachers; the Institute for Inquiry, which offers workshops about
the thory and practice of inquiry; and Community Youth Programs,
which provides programs for children, youth, and families in
partnership with community organizations. For more information,
visit exploratorium.edu.

Exploratorium® is a registered trademark and service mark
of the Exploratorium.

# Image Credits

All front and back cover images by Katrine Naleid, except back top
left (Amy Snyder [© Exploratorium]) and back top right (Cinefamily).

All interior photography by Katrine Naleid unless noted below.

p. 3: Heather Olins  pp. 8–9: Gayle Laird (© Exploratorium)
pp. 10–11: Jordan Stein (© Exploratorium)  p. 13: Nancy Rodger
(© Exploratorium)  p. 14: Susan Schwartzenberg (© Exploratorium)
p. 15: Science Photo Library  p. 21: Darren Cox  p. 22: Shutterstock
p. 23: Erin Kunkel  pp. 24–25: Cinefamily  p. 28: Shutterstock
p. 29: Shutterstock  p. 30, left: Sonya Yong James  p. 30, top and
bottom right: Shutterstock  p. 31, bottom left: Shutterstock
p. 31, top left: Paul Banday  p. 31, right: Ryo Minemizu
p. 32: Ron Hipschman  p. 35: Amy Snyder (© Exploratorium)
p. 39: iStock  p. 42, left: Shutterstock  p. 42, bottom right:
Shutterstock  p. 42, top right: NASA  p. 43, all: Shutterstock
p. 56, all: Shutterstock  p. 57, top and bottom left: Shutterstock
p. 57, right: Emily Miller  p. 61: Erin Kunkel  p. 68, left: NASA
p. 68, top right: Gianluca Lombardi  p. 68, bottom right: Shutterstock
p. 69, all: Shutterstock  p. 71: Amy Snyder (© Exploratorium)
p. 76–77: Erin Kunkel  p. 78: Shutterstock  p. 80: Nancy G. Villarroya
p. 81: Shutterstock  p. 82–83: Daniel Roberts/Gary Williams
p. 84, all: Shutterstock  p. 85, all: Shutterstock  p. 90: Heather Olins
p. 91: Amy Snyder (© Exploratorium)  p. 92, left: Rory MacLeod
p. 92, top right: Shutterstock  p. 92, bottom right: Kevin Na
p. 93, top left: Jason Kinney  p. 93, bottom left: Jon Rapp
p. 93, right: Shutterstock  p. 94: Amy Snyder (© Exploratorium)
p. 100: Colin Cameron  p. 101: Pierre-Jean Mareau  p. 104, left:
wildsingapore.com  p. 104, top and bottom right: Shutterstock
p. 105, right and top left: Shutterstock  p. 105, bottom left:
Shazaad Jasaat  pp. 106–110: Shutterstock

Illustrations by Lorraine Rath and Jenna Rosenthal.